The Actor's Book of Scenes

50 Original Comedy and Drama Scenes for Working Actors

The Actor's Book of Scenes

50 Original Comedy and Drama Scenes
for Working Actors

Mike Kimmel
Foreword by April Hartman

ISBN: 978-1-953057-19-8 (paperback)
ISBN: 978-1-953057-20-4 (ebook)

Library of Congress Control Number: 2026902995

The Actor's Book of Scenes:
50 Original Comedy and Drama Scenes for Working Actors
The Professional Actor Series: Book 6

Ben Rose Creative Arts
New York - Los Angeles

Publisher's Cataloging-in-Publication Data
provided by Five Rainbows Cataloging Services

Names: Kimmel, Mike, author. | Hartman, April, writer of foreword.
Title: The actor's book of scenes : 50 original comedy and drama scenes for working actors / Mike Kimmel.
Description: Los Angeles, CA : Ben Rose Creative Arts, 2026. | Series: Professional actor series, bk. 6.
Identifiers: LCCN 2026902995 (print) | ISBN 978-1-953057-19-8 (paperback) | ISBN 978-1-953057-20-4 (ebook)
Subjects: LCSH: Acting. | Acting--Auditioning. | Dramas. | Drama--Study and teaching. | Improvisation (Acting) | Hollywood (Los Angeles, Calif.) | BISAC: PERFORMING ARTS / Acting & Auditioning. | DRAMA / Monologues & Scenes. | EDUCATION / Arts in Education.
Classification: LCC PN2061 .K56 2026 (print) | LCC PN2061 (ebook) | DDC 792.028--dc23.
Interior design by Booknook.biz

Praise for
The Actor's Book of Scenes

"As a talent agent, I know how important it is for actors to work on their craft daily. These comedy and drama scenes have just enough subtlety and depth to allow actors to prepare themselves for real world television and film auditions. I like the back-and-forth, rapid fire dialogue too. It will help actors build their skills and confidence."

CIARRA BLACKWELL
Priority Talent Agency
Phoenix, Arizona

"Actors are always on the hunt for scenes that feel real, current, and are fun to play. *The Actor's Book of Scenes* by Mike Kimmel delivers exactly that. These scripts are packed with personality and layered relationships that give performers something meaningful to do on every page. Perfect for classes, scene study, or any time you need fresh material."

SHANNON LAINE
Actor and Producer
President, SAG-AFTRA Missouri Valley
Vice-Chair, Cinema St. Louis

"This is my favorite new book in the Mike Kimmel library. The scenes are fantastic, from the philosophical banter of 'The Waiting Room' to the sharp negotiations of 'Real Estate Shark,' offering perfect showcases for performers to demonstrate their range without extensive memorization. What makes this collection exceptional is its versatility across genres and tones, with scenes that seamlessly transition from comedy to drama and back again. The dialogue feels remarkably authentic, making these pieces perfect for any performance setting."

GIGI ERNETA
Two-time Emmy-Considered Actress
The Curse, Vindication, Veep, Flag of My Father, Duster, Dallas, Happy Death Day, Happy Death Day 2U, Outer Range, The Purge, Where You Were When, George & Tammy, Roswell, New Mexico

"Fresh, honest, and built to elevate your game. Mike Kimmel writes scenes the way good actors think, finding humor and drama in the heart of ordinary moments. His dialogue is sharp, his characters real, and every page gives performers something worth fighting for. This book belongs in every good actor's bag. Learn from a master who has done it all."

JIM BLUMETTI
Actor-Author-Acting Coach
The Alchemy of Acting: The Evolution of Craft in Film
Salem, In Plain Sight, The Good Guys, Walker, Texas Ranger, Bail Out, Altarcation, The Killer's Reprieve, Scanner Cop II

"Mike's short poignant scripts give actors an exercise that allows for no time to think but to respond authentically—giving way to a Meisner-esque approach to the craft. This attributed to a reminder that 'God gave us two ears and one mouth for a reason; listen twice as much as you speak.' Perfect to practice for cold readings."

BRIEN DIRITO
Actor-Writer-Producer
*White, Fifty, & F**k, 60 Dates in 6 Months, North Central, Angel, All of This, Murdered by Morning, Nautilus, Flooding*

"Kimmel, you've done it again! What a terrific collection of fun, fast paced scenes, perfect for those looking to sharpen their skills and have a ton of fun doing so. Comedy is so often difficult to master and find suitable material to work on, but you've provided a bible for the novice and established actors to play with.

Love the pace of some of the scenes and the simplicity, which is key when it comes to delivering interesting, sharp performances. God only knows where you come up with some of these great ideas, but keep on doing it Mike … and I'll keep on consuming!"

GLENN KEOGH
Actor
Curb Your Enthusiasm, Agents of S.H.I.E.L.D., Magnum P.I., Spiderman: No Way Home, Black Panther: Wakanda Forever, NCIS, The OA, New Girl, Ray Donovan, Scorpion, Sons of Anarchy

"Mike Kimmel has done it again! He has delivered a quality book full of fresh, slightly edgy scenes for today's actor. I love this author's style of writing. He really knows what actors need to flex their artistic muscles and show off their range of emotion and ability. This book serves up a wide variety of scenes, offering something for everyone. His writing grabs your interest from the first lines and he peppers in just the right amount of humor to layer them even further. Every actor can find something within these pages to sink their teeth into. Whether you're a professional or a budding new artist, these scenes will help you drill down into your well to find the strength or vulnerability of your voice. Kimmel's words provide lots of opportunities to show multiple colors of what you have to offer. The scenes are also great for acting class. Drama teachers, look no further. You've found a goldmine of scenes in this book! Bravo Mike Kimmel! And thank you for lending your seasoned professional talents to this collection."

JOYCE STOREY
Actor, Author, and Producer
Monologues To Go
75 New Monologues Kids Will Love!
101 Awesome Original Monologues for 20-Somethings

"There's a rhythm to the dialogue that gives actors a lot to work with in terms of pacing and intention. Nothing feels overly scripted in a stiff way. The dialogue leaves room for interpretation, which is exactly what actors need."

SCOTT OLSEN
Manhattan Book Review

"These scenes are perfect for practice in between auditions. Mike has crafted quick, relatable scenes that still offer real depth to play with. This book has become one of my favorite tools in my actor's toolbox, especially during downtime when I want to stay sharp and creatively engaged."

Sara Starr
Actor-Writer-Director
The Bunker, The Journey Back, Last Call, The Cleaning Lady

"Humor. Clever. Smart. From the creative mind of Mike Kimmel comes a catalogue of scenes that allows the actor to make their own personal choices and shine without having to honor the writer. There's a certain freedom in that, and a unique opportunity that is a gift to actors that should be relished. A veteran actor himself, Mike knows that from the moment you step on the stage, if you haven't made choices, they will be made for you. What a wonderful book that exercises both your creative and disciplined selves."

Todd Felderstein
Writer-Director-Producer
Resident Artist, The Actors Studio West
Writer: *Spider-Man* (Sony TV)
Writer-Director-Producer: *Way of the Peaceful Warrior*
(stage adaptation)

"Kimmel delivers a versatile collection of scenes spanning a wide range of themes, making this book an ideal resource for partner work and acting workshops. Each scene is intentionally crafted with space for actors to explore character, motivation, and subtext, inviting discovery with every performance. Written to be revisited again and again, the scenes transform with each new interpretation, revealing fresh emotional layers and shifting meanings. With sharp, flexible dialogue, the material can play as comedy in one reading and resonate with depth and gravity in the next."

> MISTY MARSHALL
> *American Idol:* Season 2 Semifinalist
> LA Lt. Governor's Music Commission Advisory Board
> Executive Director of Empowerment thru Arts LLC.
> Author, *The Parade at Home*

"Mike's scenes should become an essential resource in every actor's toolkit. The sharp dialogue, richly drawn characters, and comically infused scenarios provide a unique opportunity for performers to explore their craft on multiple levels. With exceptional pacing, natural delivery, and compelling character development, these scenes offer actors pure gold—material they can truly make their own. In an industry where casting directors often see the same recycled scenes, these gems not only entertain but also demonstrate a performer's ability to stand out and deliver a memorable performance."

> PAT BATTISTINI
> Actor-Director-Producer, Hoosier Daddy Films
> *Ms. Rossi, Safer at Home, Tin Can, Rebound, Tortuato,*
> *Words of Wisdom, Pushing the Boundaries, Bandwidth*

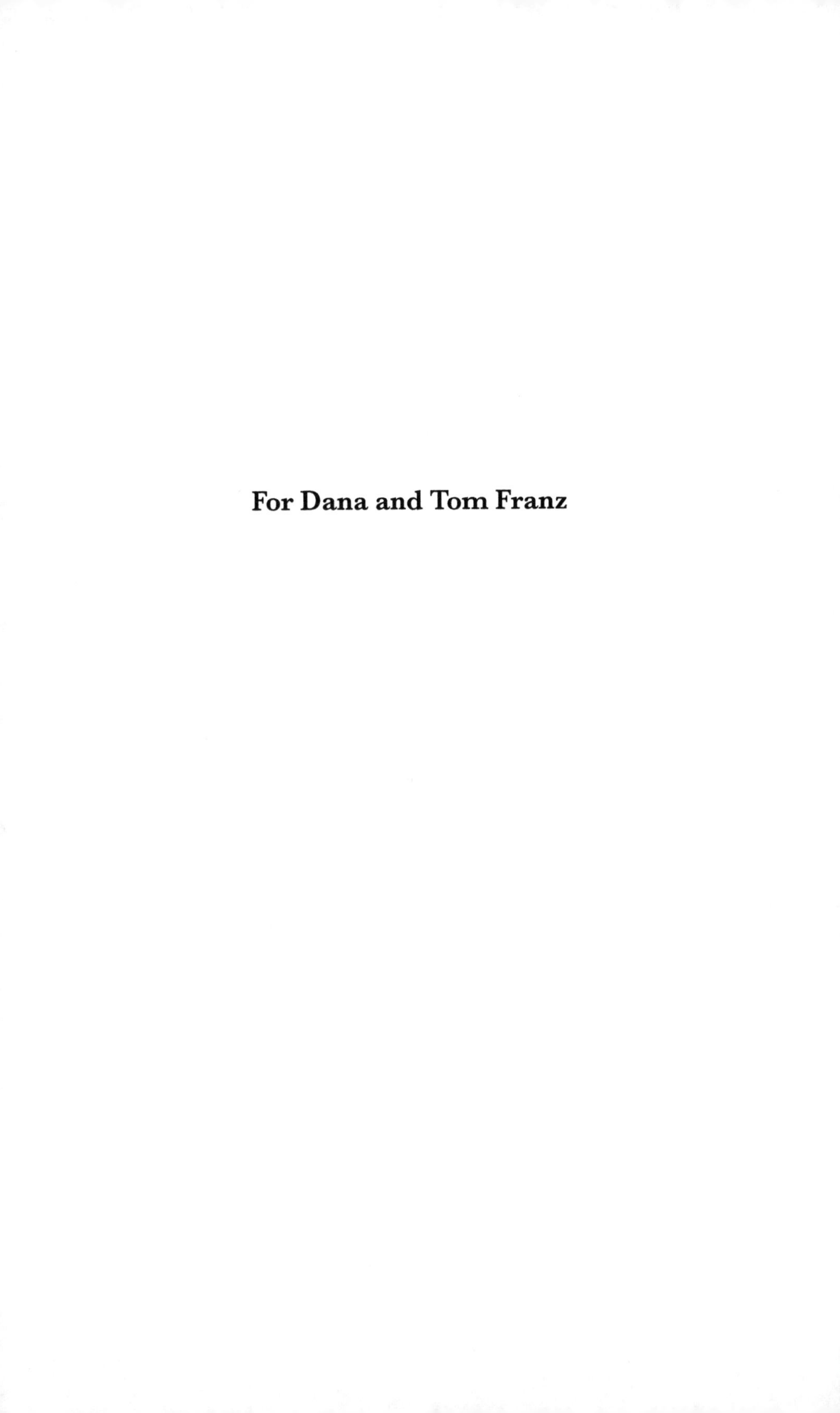

For Dana and Tom Franz

"Set out to do a good job, and do that job
so well that the living, the dead, or the
unborn couldn't do it any better."
MARTIN LUTHER KING JR.

Table of Contents

The Scenes

Appendices

"It takes twenty years to make
an overnight success."
Eddie Cantor

Foreword

I've been in this crazy, wonderful business for over twenty years now and man, it's not easy. I believe that actors are drawn to this profession. There's something inside us that feels drawn to explore human experience in its rawest, most emotional form. Through performance, we get to step into other lives, feel things deeply, and tell stories that help people feel seen, understood, or less alone. Acting is both creative release and connection—it's the thrill of transformation mixed with the challenge of vulnerability. At least, that's was always my motivation.

But let's be honest, it's not easy. It's filled with challenges and rejection. Actors are sensitive souls and we tend to take that rejection as gospel that we're not good enough. You will get a no more than a yes and the reasons you get a no have nothing to do with your talent. In short, you have to have a thick skin to stay in the game and realize, it's just the business. So let me be clear, YOU ARE ENOUGH.

It takes years of training and working to master your craft. Give yourself time and be kind to yourself. It's a journey.

I started as a little girl with a dream. I can remember as far back as five years old putting on shows and skits for my family. It was in me and it wasn't going anywhere. So, I did what most actors do, I ignored it! I remember when I was eleven, I auditioned for the Texas Girls Choir. I look back on that and I'm not sure why I did other than my mom really wanted me to. I didn't like singing and, in all honesty, I'm not good at it. But I made it in. After a few years of concerts, making records, touring and very long rehearsal days, I was done. I grew to hate it! I knew even then it wasn't feeding my soul and I grew to resent it. One day, our choir director announced that we would be doing a production of a play called *County Fair*. I reluctantly stayed in the choir to see what this was all about. I know this in my soul; that's the day I fell in love with acting. From the moment I stepped onto that stage and acted for the first time, I knew it was something special. I was hooked!

Life happened and I walked away from acting again but this time, with the exception of a couple of school plays, it would be fifteen years before I returned. See, it always pulls you back! I got serious this time and started training immediately. I got an agent and got to work!

I understand how fortunate I've been in this business. Through the years I've worked in some exceptional places with some amazing people. From leads in feature films to TV series to national commercials, it's been quite a ride. One that I wouldn't trade for anything.

Throughout my acting years I've learned two things that I think are the most important in show business. First, train/learn every day! Work on your craft! Learn a skill, another language, an accent, anything. Work on something that will help you grow as an artist and a person every single day. It will make your work rich and layered with authenticity, and that's what people want to see.

The second most important, FIND YOUR PEOPLE Meaning, the people that are willing to help you grow, share their insights

---

Work on your craft! Learn a skill, another language, an accent, anything. Work on something that will help you grow as an artist and a person every single day.

---

and experiences with you and that truly believe in you. Surround yourself with these people and your journey will be fruitful.

I moved to Albuquerque in 2022. The first thing on my agenda was to find my people. I wanted to immerse myself in the acting scene and find out who was making waves in the local industry, the people who are killing the game. I started attending networking events, going to plays, workshops, whatever I could do to find my people. Shortly after I arrived, I started holding my own networking events. It was at one of these events that I met Mike. I knew immediately that he was a force!

Mike Kimmel is one of my people. From that first time that I had a conversation with Mike, I knew that he would not only be a colleague but a trusted friend. Mike never hesitates to share what he knows from his years of success. He encourages me when I'm down on myself. He lifts me up when I become a brat actor and pout that I didn't book something or I'm just not getting enough auditions. He understands. What truly makes Mike special is his desire to help everyone. He not only understands how hard this business is, but also how much actors pour their souls into their work. Mike really loves his fellow actors and that love manifests in helping them gain knowledge they need to be successful and

---

There's no longer an excuse that you don't have material to practice; it's right here!

---

materials for them to stay in shape. For years he's been passing on his knowledge and helping those around him. I am so grateful to him for realizing the need for this information and putting it out there. I'm excited for this book and for actors everywhere to utilize it. There's no longer an excuse that you don't have material to practice; it's right here!

Mike, thank you for your friendship. Thank you for your guidance and unending support. I'm so proud of you and all your achievements. No one deserves it more. In this dark world, you are a ray of sunshine!

Your friend always,

APRIL HARTMAN
ALBUQUERQUE, NEW MEXICO

Actors, get to work!

Acknowledgments

As always, a million thanks to my wonderful family—my sisters, their husbands, their children, and children's children—for always being there for me.

Many thanks to Tracey Adlai, Holly Anderson, Ciarra Blackwell, Susannah Devereux, Kimber Eastwood, GiGi Erneta, Tina and A.J. Guillot, Misty Marshall, Sara Starr, Joyce Storey, Pat Battistini, Jim Blumetti, David Breland, Case Copeland, Francis Ford Coppola, Brien DiRito, Chuck Disney, Todd Felderstein, Freddie Ganno, Christopher Jones, Glenn Keogh, Ben McCain, Butch McCain, Ben Rose, and William Wellman Jr. for their friendship, encouragement, inspiration, and support throughout the writing process.

Very special thanks to my dear friend and colleague, April Hartman, for taking the time to write such a thoughtful and impactful foreword for this book. April is an absolute force of nature—a super-talented actor, writer, director, producer, and teacher. She is also one of the kindest, most creative, and hardest-working people I've ever met. I'm grateful for our years of friendship and look forward to many more collaborations in the years ahead.

"The way to do anything is to begin."
William James

Introduction

Thank you for selecting this book. I hope ***The Actor's Book of Scenes*** will be a valuable resource you can use and apply throughout your acting career. One of the most strategic things you can do as an actor is to commit yourself daily to practicing our craft with a variety of scenes and monologues. There is a wide assortment of scenes in this collection, encompassing both comedy and drama. I hope you will find several that resonate with you—and allow you to show off your skill set to best advantage.

There is also a variation in the length of the scenes included. The longer scenes will be most helpful for actors mainly interested in theater, while the shorter scenes will generally work best for those interested in television and film. No matter what your primary interest, however, it's always useful to vary your training with a variety of scenes of different lengths and styles. It's also important for actors to train themselves to work in both mediums—on stage and on screen.

Working actors in our industry may receive audition scripts that are five to seven pages in length. Then, a week later, they may be asked to read for a much smaller part—sometimes even a one-line or two-line role.

Adaptability is key. Show business demands extraordinary flexibility. Actors who are able to seamlessly go from reading longer scenes to shorter scenes, comedy scenes to drama scenes, and even performing scenes of an abstract nature—scenes they don't fully understand—are at a tremendous advantage. These are the actors best able to maintain long-term careers in the entertainment industry.

Don't concern yourself too much with whether the scene you select for practice is a comedy or a drama scene. Some scenes in theater, television, and film have elements of both and are difficult to classify. Some scenes are also known in our industry as "informational scenes." These are scenes placed into a script simply to provide important information that helps move the storyline forward. We see this most often in murder mysteries, thrillers, and daytime dramas.

A Note on Nervousness and Stage Fright

Most people are surprised to learn that many of their favorite actors—and even our biggest stars—still struggle with stage fright and nervousness. These feelings and fears can affect actors at all levels in our industry; they are not only reserved for the newcomers.

Academy Award winner Marlon Brando said it best: "I put on an act sometimes, and people think I'm insensitive. Really, it's like a kind of armor because I'm too sensitive. If there are two hundred people in a room and one of them doesn't like me, I've got to get out." Dorothy Dandridge echoed these sentiments, declaring: "If one person in a thousand criticized me while all the others cheered, I didn't hear the cheers."

Recognize that this is a never-ending battle—and a battle you can win each day. Practice doesn't make perfect, but it builds a skill set that allows confidence in the area you're practicing to

Practice doesn't make perfect, but it builds a skill set that allows confidence in the area you're practicing to slowly emerge.

slowly emerge. As your confidence and adaptability build, these qualities will begin to replace your nervousness. The nervousness may still be there—and may continue throughout your career—but it will progressively become smaller, edged out, or pushed to the side. Eventually, you will also focus on it less because you will now be paying greater attention to your emerging skill set—simply through force of daily habit. That's why it's so important to practice with a variety of scenes and monologues each day. With time, you will find, as most experienced actors do, that you will begin to notice your nervousness and self-consciousness far less frequently, as well.

My old teacher Michael Shurtleff—author of the book *Audition*—used to say that he thought of actors preparing to go out on stage like racehorses warming up in the paddock right before the starting gate opens. I always loved this analogy. While many acting teachers advise their students to relax and breathe deeply—Mr. Shurtleff encouraged us to use our nervous energy to propel us forward into the scene. As the old saying goes, the goal is not to get rid of the butterflies in your stomach—but to get all those butterflies flying in formation.

A Note on the Writing of these Scripts

Some of these dialogues are shorter; some are longer. That's how our conversations in everyday life work too—and these scenes are meant to mirror real life conversations. In real life, we often talk in a familiar shorthand with one another. We do not feel the need to express ourselves in full sentences with the people closest to us.

The goal for actors should always be to read and practice these scenes so naturally that—when you're rehearsing with a scene partner—anyone watching will think it's a real conversation between two real people. It should look like a natural conversation unfolding right before the viewer's eyes in real time. It must always seem real to the audience. George Bernard Shaw said it best: "The function of the actor is to make the audience imagine for the moment that real things are happening to real people."

It should look like a natural conversation unfolding right before the viewer's eyes in real time. It must always seem real to the audience.

While an acting script must be realistic, it's not real life exactly —that would be a little bit too mundane for our viewers. People watch television at night and go to the movies on weekends to escape from their normal, work-a-day lives. Acting scripts, then, should always have an underlying exaggeration woven through the dialogue. It's what we call a "heightened reality." Alfred Hitchcock said it best: "Drama is life with the dull bits cut out."

Bette Davis took Hitchcock's idea one step further, declaring: "Acting should be bigger than life. Scripts should be bigger than life. It should all be bigger than life."

But there are limits to exaggeration, as well. There must always be a balance. Garry Marshall explained this principle brilliantly. The legendary writer-director-producer often said that writers can place an over-the-top character in a real life setting … or a realistic character in an exaggerated setting … but they can't have an over-the-top character in an exaggerated setting. The result would be a cartoonish character that audiences would not find believable. Ann Loring, an old friend, wonderful actor, and early writing teacher of mine, had a beautiful way of describing this idea. "It's a little bit much of a muchness," Ann used to say.

Besides exaggeration, though, there's also the risk that a scene will explain too much. "Show, don't tell" is a commonly heard warning in television writing rooms. Don't insult your audience's intelligence by telling them every little detail. Yes, writers must be specific, but they should always leave room for a little purposeful ambiguity. There's often more power in what's left unsaid rather than what is spelled out in minute detail. Additionally, scripts become much more interesting when you leave room for a double meaning. This is best accomplished by dropping subtle cues—and carefully weaving subtext through our scenes. When writers do this, they give the audience opportunities to become more engaged in the storyline—and debate story points that are open to interpretation.

Writer-producer Vince Gilligan had a wonderful take on this subject. "Let the audience put two and two together so that it comes up with four," Mr. Gilligan said. "Let then do that themselves and they'll love you forever."

I hope you'll love the scripts in this book forever. I hope you'll use them to hone your skills, boost your confidence, and knock your auditions out of the park. If you find that it helps you to change a script detail—such as a location, character name, or occupation—then please feel free to do so. I often tell my readers and students: "It's my book, but it's your audition." Please feel free to modify these scripts as necessary to suit your own unique personality and background. You're the world's greatest living expert on you.

I wish you all the very best on your actor's journey—and every other journey you will take in life.

Now go get 'em.

MIKE KIMMEL
ALBUQUERQUE, NEW MEXICO

The Scenes

The Waiting Room

A Have you been waiting long?

B I think so.

A You think so?

B Time is relative, but it has still lost all sense of meaning for me.

A I'll take that as a yes.

B Thank you. When we learn to become comfortable with the uncomfortable situations in our lives … only then do we achieve true self-mastery.

A That's great. Are you here for an oil change?

B Yes. It's an essential part of the renewal process. Out with the old. In with the new.

A That's right. Keeping up with oil changes is the life of your engine. When was the last time you rotated your tires?

B I don't remember. The presidential election, I believe.

A Wanna throw that in? Twenty bucks.

B Excellent suggestion.

A Are we using the high viscosity motor oil?

B Is that recommended for my vehicle?

A I think so.

B Then yes, by all means.

A We have a very nice customer waiting area. Coffee. Donuts. The works.

B That's very thoughtful. My congratulations to you and the entire team.

A It's the little things that count. Take care of the little things
and the big things take care of themselves.

B Remarkable. That was my father's favorite expression!

A Was he in the car business too?

B He invented the electron microscope.

Hole in My Schedule

A   What's on my schedule?

B   Nothing. Nothing until three.

A   You're my assistant. How could that be?

B   Miller canceled and Blavatsky's still in Houston.

A   Houston? In Texas?

B   Unless they moved it.

A   Don't get smart with me. What's he doing in Houston? Nobody goes to Houston. It's too crowded.

B   Not his fault. Connecting flight got canceled.

A   It is his fault. He knows better. He should have booked a direct flight.

B   Maybe. Airlines are hurting. Airlines are canceling flights.

A   He should have been on the flight before the one that got canceled. Then he'd be here early, do a little extra prep before our meeting, and be ready to make me money when I say "jump."

B   Maybe he needs to plan a little better.

A   Gotta plan a little better. Nobody makes millions with a hundred dollar work ethic.

B   That's a good one.

A   Yes. Write that down. Text it to me. We'll put it in the next book.

B   Will do.

A And why the hell did Miller cancel?

B He didn't say.

A Find out. He doesn't cancel on me, I cancel on him.

B I'll let him know.

A Good. I do not accept holes in my schedule. Nature abhors a vacuum.

B I'll let him know.

A You do that.

B I will.

Personal Assistant

A How's my schedule?

B Booked solid.

A Good. What am I doing for dinner?

B Film screening with Jacobson's team. They'll have finger foods.

A Gluten free?

B I think so.

A Find out.

B Will do.

A Do I like their project?

B I'm leaning towards "yes."

A Don't get smart with me. I don't pay you for your personality.

B Sorry.

A Continue.

B Jacobson's project is now fully funded.

A Am I interested?

B Yes. Same team they worked with at Paramount.

A I don't like it. One success makes everyone lazy. Cut corners. Overlook important details.

B That's true. Human nature.

A Human nature shouldn't have to cost me money. Call me one hour in. Might have to make a fast getaway.

B Will do.

A Good. Anything else?

B Not today.

A How about you? You happy?

B Yes.

A Fulfilled?

B Completely.

A How's the job? Hours? Workload? Stress level? Parking?

B Wonderful. All systems go.

A Good. Am I paying you enough?

B Almost.

A When's your next performance review?

B Six months.

A Six months is no good. Give yourself another thousand.

B Monthly?

A Annually.

Bidding War

A Did you see my email?

B I saw you sent something, but I didn't read it.

A That's the whole point of sending it. For you to read it.

B Listen, I know what it's about and I'm not interested.

A You should be. There's gonna be a bidding war.

B You sure about that?

A Sure about that.

B Might want to check your crystal ball. I disagree. It's over-valued and the timing is terrible.

A You're gonna lose out if you don't move quickly on this one.

B How can I lose out on something I'm not interested in?

A Might want to modify what you're interested in.

B No thanks. You don't bring a baseball bat to a football game.

A Depends who you're playing. We're in a full-contact industry these days. No rewards for players who stand on the sidelines.

B No bankruptcy filings, either.

A Try looking at the big picture. We'll have ten bids minimum as soon as I say "Go." They'll be lining up around the block.

B Good for them. They can have my place in line. They can have it with my blessings.

A Okay. You sure I can't talk you into this?

B I'm sure you can't talk me into this.

A I just hate to see you miss out on a great opportunity.

B If it's that great an opportunity, they don't need my bid. I can put my money elsewhere.

A Elsewhere where?

B A less crowded elsewhere.

A Okay, if you say so. I'll stop asking.

B Yes, I say so. Please stop asking.

Real Estate Shark

A How much is it?

B They listed it at five hundred forty thousand.

A Do you think they'd accept six hundred? I hate writing a check for an odd amount.

B You are friggin' hilarious.

A I aim to please.

B I'm pleased that you aim.

A Touché. I knew I wasn't wasting my time with you.

B Seriously. Are you interested in the house?

A How long has it been on the market?

B Three weeks.

A Any bites?

B Nibbles mostly. Not too many showings at this price point.

A Maybe it's priced high.

B No. I ran comps. It's right in the middle. Lot of nice upgrades too.

A Well … it's early yet. Takes some buyers three weeks to put on their shoes.

B We had one couple that was very interested, but they couldn't secure financing.

A Tell them to pay their bills on time. Stop eating in restaurants. Eliminate their car payments and credit card debt.

B A lot of people can't handle that discipline. Livin' for the moment.

A It's called adulting. When you chase every shiny new object, you lose track of what you really want at the end of the rainbow.

B That's a lot of wisdom. I'm getting a lot of wisdom here today.

A Good. Write that down and burn it.

B Back to the house. Can I write up an offer? Full price?

A I don't pay full price for coffee and a donut.

B Five-forty is a good deal.

A Five hundred cash. No points. No closing costs. No back-talk.

B How high can we go when they counter?

A No counter. Five hundred. Best and final.

B I think my friend is becoming a real estate shark.

A That's me. Run when you're wrong. Fight when you're right.

I Met Someone

A Did I tell you I met someone?

B No! Good for you! That's wonderful!

A I think so.

B What do you mean, "You think so?"

A Not sure where it's going.

B Did you go out yet?

A Not exactly.

B Uh … that's a yes or no question. Dating has a short menu.

A No. But I got digits. I got a number.

B That's good. That's progress.

A But I think it's not the right number. I get a voicemail saying the number I'm calling is restricted.

B Did you try texting?

A No response. I think it's not going through.

B Where did you meet this Mystery Date?

A Post office.

B In line?

A No. Works behind the counter.

B Good looking?

A Exceptionally. And we always have these great conversations.

B   At the counter in the post office?

A   Yeah, but I don't want to be too obvious … and I can't stay too long at the counter talking when there's a line. It's a little awkward.

B   Sounds a lot awkward.

A   It's becoming increasingly awkward.

B   How did you get digits?

A   I wrote "Coffee?" on the back of an envelope … then drew two boxes and "Check Yes or No."

B   You got a "Yes."

A   I got a "Yes." Then I handed over the pen.

B   So your postal employee could transcribe digits.

A   Correct.

B   But the digits are incorrect.

A   Also correct.

B   What happens when you go to the post office now?

A   Avoids me. Runs to the back. Doesn't wait on me any more.

B   You might need to widen your circle. Start expanding your borders and boundaries.

A   You mean look for someone else to date?

B   Correct. And you might need to find yourself a new post office.

Have We Met?

A Excuse me. Have we met?

B I don't think so.

A I could swear we've met somewhere before.

B Never been there.

A I'm sure we've met.

B No. I'm sure I would remember that.

A Maybe in a work situation … a work environment … a conference of some sort … a couple of months back?

B I work alone.

A Sounds like fun. Wish I could work alone.

B A blessing and a curse.

A Sounds like my first marriage.

B That's why I work alone.

A Sounds like my second marriage.

B That's a good one. You're pretty funny.

A Appreciate it.

B Appreciate the humor. Miles of smiles.

A Well … my mistake.

B No harm, no foul.

A Enjoy your day.

B And you, as well.

A Uh … this is crazy, but …

B Do I want to get a cup of coffee?

A I was thinking Chai tea.

B Well, that's a nice surprise.

A Balance is key. Tai Chi in the morning. Chai tea in the afternoon. In the evening, the twain shall meet.

B Deal. You can introduce yourself over Chai tea.

A Perfect.

B Then we'll have met.

I Like Your Watch

A Excuse me. What time do you have?

B Half past four.

A Thanks.

B Welcome.

A Oh … I like that watch.

B Thanks.

A Welcome. How much?

B Beg pardon?

A How much do you want for it?

B Uh … it's not for sale.

A Might be my favorite watch ever. Give me a number. We can do this. Let's transact.

B No, thank you.

A How much did you pay? I'll triple it.

B It was a gift.

A Fine. Take the money and buy three new ones.

B Uh … no. My better half would not appreciate that.

A I can be extremely persuasive.

B Not with me. Maybe you should find a new favorite watch.

A Maybe you should find a new better half.

B Nah. I'm kinda used to the one I have.

A How long have you been married?

B Longer than I can remember. I might have been born married.

A Are you head over heels in love?

B Like I said. I'm kinda used to the one I have.

A Ah, yes. Wedded bliss.

B Yeah. Something like that.

A Maybe you two lovebirds would like some company tonight. Three's my favorite number.

B That's my cue.

A Don't be in such a hurry.

B Excuse me. I have business to attend to back on Planet Earth.

A Yum. One of my favorite planets. Hotter than Venus. Cooler than Mars.

B Hotter than something.

A Wait until I get warmed up.

B Seems like you're already warmed up.

A Just wait until you get to know me better.

B No, thank you. It's been fun, but I'd better get going.

A Headed home to that head-over-heels better half?

B Yes. Same better half who walked me down the aisle.

A Ah, yes. Wedded bliss.

B Maybe not head over heels. But comfortable, familiar … and loyal.

A Loyalty versus temptation.

B That's one way to put it.

A I guess loyalty counts for something these days.

B It counts for a lot in my world. Back here on Planet Earth.

Still Single. Seeking Double.

A   How you doing?

B   Hey.

A   Good to see you.

B   Yeah.

A   Do you hear something?

B   No.

A   That's funny, because I'm talking to you.

B   Stop. I'm not in a mood.

A   Come on. What's going on with you lately?

B   I don't know. In a funk, I guess.

A   About what?

B   Just life.

A   It beats the alternative.

B   Yeah. How many people do you know like us?

A   Great looking, smart, strong, dynamic, ambitious, friendly, and capable?

B   Single.

A   Ah … that too.

B   How many of our friends from college are still single?

A   Including you and me?

B Yeah.

A Two.

B Never thought I'd still be single at this stage of my life.

A Single's not so bad.

B Thought I'd be double by now.

A Well … it's not for lack of trying. You've definitely been getting yourself out there.

B Been meeting people … but no chemistry.

A If there's no chemistry, there's not gonna be any biology.

B Tell me about it.

A I just did.

B Nice.

A Being single's nice too. It depends on your mindset.

B Maybe you're right.

A There's lots of married people who'd like to trade places with us.

B Yeah, I sure know a few of those.

A So? Are we close to getting you out of that funk?

B I don't know. I guess it's a process.

A Every process starts with an action. What can we do right now?

B Lunch would be nice.

A Favorite burger place?

B Sure thing. I'm buying.

A Throw in a beer and you've got yourself a deal.

B I stopped drinking.

A I just started.

The Sales Call

A You're back.

B In a manner of speaking.

A How did it go with Santini's father?

B Not sure.

A You didn't close?

B Couldn't close him. Tough nut.

A He's a tough nut, all right. Santini's tough enough. The father's damn near impossible.

B Glad you warned me about him.

A No worries. We've been trying to close that guy for years.

B I'll go back in two weeks. Got a feeling I'll close him then.

A That's the spirit.

B Follow the money.

A There's plenty of it there.

B I could smell it on him. He's a whale, for sure.

A Big commission for the rep who can close him.

B And any client—

A Potential client.

B Fine. Potential client. Any potential client with that much cash has learned a few things about finance.

A Correct. Learned how to protect that money pile.

B Make sure it doesn't walk.

A So how do we close him?

B Change his game plan from defense to offense. Show him how big that mountain of cash can grow.

A With our help. I like it.

B Easier to turn a million into a billion than a thousand into a million.

A You got that right. Seen it happen a million times.

B Billion times. They don't name universities after people who hide their money in coffee cans.

A Risk versus reward.

B Two out of three falls. No time limit. And when I go back for round two …

A … with Santini's father …

B I'm gonna teach Poppa Bear to think bigger.

The Doctor's Visit

A Thanks for seeing me on such short notice, doctor.

B That's why I came to this planet. What brings you in today?

A I was working out in my backyard—

B Good for you! Exercise! Sunshine! Fresh air!

A Then a bee came out of nowhere and stung me. Now it's swelling up real bad.

B Where is it?

A I don't know. It flew away. Must have scared it when I screamed.

B No! Where on your body?! Where did it sting you?

A Oh! Upper arm. Right below this tattoo.

B Let's have a look.

A What do you think? Bad?

B Nah. I saw worse in Afghanistan. Let's clean her up a little. Fresh bandage. Any allergies?

A No, I don't think so.

B Pollen? Dander? Gluten?

A All clear.

B Medications?

A None.

B Any history of anxiety or depression?

A Not until today.

B Alcohol swab and a mild anti-inflammatory are all you need. You'll be good as new in a day or two. Don't let this one incident sour you on the great outdoors.

A Might have to invest in a beekeepers' suit before I do any more outdoor workouts.

B It'll look good on you. Fresh air and outdoor exercise are great for clearing the mind, body, and spirit. We all need to spend more time outdoors after being stuck inside and isolated for so long with that pandemic.

A I guess you're right.

B Trust me. I went to school for this.

A Good point.

B Take one day at a time.

A Okay.

B That's why they put them on the calendar consecutively.

A Useful Mnemonic Device

A I'm thinking I have something kinda important to tell you.

B Okay.

A But I forgot what it was.

B It'll come back.

A Like a boomerang?

B Sure. When was the last time you thought of it?

A Thought of what?

B The thing you can't remember.

A I can't remember.

B Okay. I have a useful mnemonic device that may come in handy.

A What is it?

B Sometimes when I forget something, I go back to the spot I was standing in the last time I remembered it.

A Remembered what?

B What I forgot.

A That's a good idea.

B Thank you.

A You're welcome.

B So … where were you standing?

A Who?

B You.

A When?

B When you remembered what you forgot.

A I'll have to think about that.

B That's a good idea.

A Thank you.

B You're welcome.

A Guess what?

B What?

A I think it's coming back now.

B Told you. Just like a boomerang.

A I'm thinking maybe I wanted to ask you to borrow two hundred dollars until payday.

B Are you sure that's it?

A Pretty sure that's it. Two hundred dollars. Maybe three hundred dollars would be better so I don't have to ask you again.

B Tell you what.

A What?

B Let's forget we ever had this conversation.

A What conversation?

B Exactly.

My Future Self

A Hey, a bunch of us are going out for pizza and a late movie. Wanna join us?

B No, I've got an early call.

A I thought you were off tomorrow.

B I am, but I have an early morning appointment.

A With who?

B My future self.

A Wanna run that by me again?

B Sure. I have an early morning strategy session with my future self. The version of me that I want to become someday.

A How does this work exactly?

B We get together once a week. Me and the Ten-Year-Older-Version of Me. I ask questions. I look at all the accomplishments the Ten-Year-Older-Me has made and then we reverse engineer the processes I can use now to get there.

A Just the two of you?

B Sometimes three. Twenty-Year-Older Me shows up to join us sometimes too. That's when we really get the heavy lifting done.

A Okay. Let me get this straight. You're passing up an invitation with all your friends to hang out with fictitious characters from your imagination.

B They're not fictitious. They're the best possible versions of myself that I'm actively speaking into existence through creative visualization. And we're not hanging out, we're working.

A Where did you get this idea?

B It's closely related to Napoleon Hill's idea of creating a master-mind group for dream building and goal attainment.

A Napoleon Hill? *Think and Grow Rich?*

B Yes, that's his best known book, but he wrote quite of bit of other material in the self-help and personal development field. Sometimes he joins us in our strategy meetings.

A Napoleon Hill joins you?

B Yes. He helps moderate.

A Can't you meet with these guys in the library during normal business hours?

B It's my social calendar and I'll fill it up or clear it out as I see fit.

A What's that they say about all work and no play?

B I don't know. I was working when they were playing.

A Gotta admit, that's a good one. Can I bring you back some pizza? You still have to eat.

B Sure thing. That'd be great.

A Got it. Should I bring some pizza for your future self?

B No, thanks. Future Me is gluten free.

Can I See the Manager?

A You asked for a manager?

B Yes, that was me.

A What seems to be the trouble?

B Where should I begin?

A At the beginning.

B I made an appointment three weeks ago, your technicians are running two hours behind, your customer service is non-existent, and there's no coffee or donuts in the customer waiting area.

A We're unusually busy. We had two employees call out sick today.

B I made this appointment three weeks ago.

A You said that already.

B Is it possible to move me up in the schedule?

A It's not possible. We had two emergency jobs that required extra attention. They came in yesterday, but could not be completed the same day.

B Shouldn't you give priority to the earlier-scheduled appointments?

A I'm afraid not. That's not our policy.

B And why is that?

A We give priority to the emergency jobs that come in unexpectedly. That's why they're called emergencies.

B That's not acceptable. I'm taking this up the chain. I'm going to complain to the district manager.

A I'm very sorry to hear that.

B I didn't enjoy saying it.

A Thank you.

B It's ridiculous. I made this appointment three weeks ago.

A You said that already. We're talking in circles.

B This is the last time you'll see me and my credit card.

A I'm very sorry to hear that.

B You said that already. We're talking in circles.

A I'm sorry we couldn't help you today.

B No, you're not.

A May I make one minor suggestion?

B Yes. Please.

A You might want to cut back on the donuts.

Ghosting vs. Dealing

A   What's going on with you?

B   What do you mean?

A   Been trying to call you all day.

B   Had my phone off. Trying to avoid a couple of people right now.

A   Uh-huh. A little ghosting.

B   I guess you could call it that.

A   Because it is that?

B   Uh … yeah.

A   Did you ever think—

B   —I always think.

A   Did you ever think … you might want to work on your social skills?

B   My social skills?

A   Yes. You shouldn't just write people off.

B   Some people need to be written off.

A   That's a sure sign of immaturity.

B   A sign of immaturity?!

A   You've got to learn to talk things out. Learn to confront people when they're crossing a line in your life. Let them know why it's not okay. That's maturity.

B Not sure I can control my temper.

A That's immaturity. Don't be so dramatic. You can control your temper.

B If I don't ghost 'em, I may kill 'em. Then I'll be ghosting them by default.

A You know you don't mean that.

B Don't be so sure. These people really crossed the line. They really did me wrong.

A When was the last time you hauled off and hit someone who did you wrong?

B Including last summer at the beach resort?

A Yeah.

B Maybe … fifteen, twenty years ago.

A Uh-huh. I think you can control your temper.

B Maybe you're right.

A Trust me. Just deal with people as they are. Nobody's had an easy time of it these last couple of years.

B Including me, I guess.

A Know what that sounds like?

B I think you're gonna tell me.

A A sure sign of maturity.

Going Backward. Going Forward.

A I'm thinking about going back with my ex.

B Don't do it.

A You don't think it's a good idea?

B Negatory.

A We were good together once upon a time.

B What year was this?

A Not so long ago.

B No?

A Well, okay. Maybe it was long ago. But things were pretty great.

B Great? I think we need to define "great."

A I'd say it was great up until …

B I remember.

A That one event.

B Don't even say it.

A Okay, but we could have … maybe worked that out. Maybe.

B Uh-huh. Pretty big event.

A Yeah. Okay. It was big.

B And I seem to remember a great deal of chaos and drama in that relationship.

A Maybe so.

B I remember many four-hour conversations with you … trying to help you get your life back. And talk you off the ledge. Remember?

A Kinda sorta.

B And many trips to the bank, motor vehicle bureau, police department, and credit repair company to put Humpty Dumpty back together again.

A But …

B But what?

A Life's not supposed to be so lonely.

B And life's too short to go backwards.

A Maybe.

B Maybe what?

A Maybe you're right.

B Maybe I'm right?

A But maybe we're both older and wiser now.

B Maybe. And maybe … how quickly they forget.

Impartial Third Party Observer

A You're late.

B Good to see you too. Been a little worried.

A Worried about me? Why?

B I understand you saw your ex.

A Yes, I saw my ex. No, you don't understand.

B Enlighten me.

A My ex had a very bad habit.

B Yeah? What was it?

A Liked to collect glass bottles. Our home was full of them.

B Doesn't sound so bad.

A Drank all the whiskey out of those glass bottles first.

B Ah … got it.

A Trying to be kind. "Collecting glass bottles" sounds a lot better than calling the love of my life a raging alcoholic.

B You have mastered the art of euphemism.

A Yes. I have developed that skill through many years of painful repetition.

B And how might one apply that acquired knowledge?

A Beg pardon?

B How does a thinking person turn painful experience into practical application?

A For the betterment of humanity?

B Sure. But maybe just for the benefit of yourself.

A Good question.

B And the answer?

A I don't know.

B If you don't know, who's gonna know?

A I don't know.

B I do.

A You do?

B I do.

A Enlighten me, then.

B As an impartial third party observer, I can tell you there's a lesson to be learned here.

A I'm all ears.

B Learn to love the sound of your own feet as they walk away from things that are not meant for you.

A That's … profound.

B Fall in love with your footsteps. Let them become the new love of your life.

A Wow. That's intense. In other words … don't invite chaos back into my life.

B Show chaos the door. Here endeth the lesson.

The Different One

A Did you ever feel like the different one?

B Uh … I'm not sure.

A Like you're the odd person out. The one who doesn't quite belong.

B I think I don't quite belong in this conversation.

A Come on. Think. It's not illegal yet.

B Yeah, yeah, okay. I think I know what you mean.

A Did you ever walk into a room full of people …

B And feel all alone?

A Exactly!

B And wonder why I'm the odd one out.

A How you got there.

B And how do I get out.

A Right.

B Like I'm a guest at someone else's high school reunion.

A Yes! That's a good way of putting it!

B Yeah, I think everybody feels like that from time to time.

A So how come nobody ever talks about it?

B I don't know.

A If you don't know, who's gonna know?

B I don't know.

A Well, I'm telling you, this is a common experience. There's a commonality of human experience across all cultures and civilizations. We are one.

B But it's so uncomfortable … feeling like you're the odd one out.

A The discomfort is universal. It connects us all together worldwide.

B Can't we find something better to connect us together worldwide?

A I don't know.

B If you don't know, who's gonna know?

A I don't know.

B Maybe that's our commonality of human experience.

A Right. Everybody feels that way.

B And nobody knows why.

A And nobody even talks about it.

B And everybody's walking around feeling like they don't quite belong.

A Like a guest at someone else's high school reunion.

No Substitutions

A Coffee?

B Reading my mind.

A That's why they pay me the big bucks.

B My Uncle Billy made big bucks. About an eighth of an inch too big. He's doing time now.

A Ah, so they finally caught Uncle Billy.

B Bound to happen sooner or later. Always getting in trouble playing blackjack at the casino. Has to get completely naked to count to twenty-one.

A Sorry, only the wait staff are allowed to make bad jokes here.

B Oh! I didn't see the sign.

A Okay, that's it. I'm cutting you off.

B Thought only bartenders can do that.

A Restaurant employees have a special dispensation.

B Is that right?

A Yep. Just passed the legislature.

B Okay, I'll behave. Any chance I can order some food?

A Every chance. We aim to please.

B Wonderful. I'll have a BLT please. Not too greasy.

A Sorry. Not on our menu.

B   No worries. Very easy to prepare. I'm sure your chef can make that happen for me, right?

A   No can do. No changes. No substitutions.

B   It's easy. Take the bacon from your breakfast special. Take the lettuce and tomato from your hamburger deluxe. Slap 'em together between two slices of lightly toasted bread and we're in business.

A   I'm all business. Our menu clearly states, "No substitutions."

B   Whatever happened to the customer is always right?

A   Not in this case. Our menus can't be changed.

B   Why not?

A   We just had them laminated.

B   What if I write on it with a permanent marker?

A   We'd have you arrested for defacing private property.

B   Might be worth it.

A   Why's that?

B   I'll get to see Uncle Billy again.

A   Good. Tell Uncle Billy I said hello. Tell him to come see us when he gets out of the slammer.

B   Will do.

A   And ask him to make you a BLT. Not too greasy.

Backwards in Time

A   What's up with you?

B   Nothing.

A   Looks like something.

B   Just a little out of sorts these days. In a bit of a funk.

A   Got a feeling everyone is.

B   Wish I could jump back in time.

A   To when?

B   A kinder, gentler, simpler society. When life was much less complex. Fewer choices and options.

A   I'm not sure that time period ever existed.

B   Way back. My grandparents' day.

A   World War I. Spanish flu. Great Depression. World War II.

B   Okay, my parents' time then.

A   Viet Nam. Civil Rights movement. John F. Kennedy assassination. Martin Luther King assassination. Robert F. Kennedy assassination.

B   Okay! Okay! Then way, way back. Maybe before we had all this technology. Cowboy days. Caveman days.

A   Cavemen had the T-Rex. Stegosaurus. Volcanos. Meteors and asteroids hurtling towards the Earth. On a good day, cavemen only had to deal with sabre-toothed tigers.

B   There's bows and arrows for that.

A   That was their new technology. Cavemen probably had a steep learning curve.

B   Well … maybe you got something there.

A   Lots of resistance to the new technology. Lots of cavemen would have liked to stick to their trusty old clubs and spears.

B   Yeah. Guess I can relate.

A   And don't even get me started on the wheel.

B   Maybe you're right. No wheel, no Lambo.

The Department Head

A Good afternoon, Professor.

B I understand you had a question about the syllabus.

A Yes. Is this the syllabus for the entire semester?

B This is what Professor Barrow has been following for the better part of twenty years.

A Excuse me for asking, but it seems a bit light, doesn't it?

B Professor Barrow was very definite. He insisted his replacement follow this syllabus to the letter until his return.

A Honestly, though, I taught a high school class in this subject area with more references and … far more comprehensive content.

B I suppose we'll just have to humor him.

A Well, you're the Department Head. I'll do it your way, of course. But I'm quite surprised at the thinness of the material … the lack of quality content for a college course.

B I agree with you.

A Good. You agree that the syllabus leaves much to be desired?

B No. I agree that I'm the Department Head. And you'll do it my way. Of course.

A Oh, okay. Yes … I see.

B We understand each other, then?

A Yes, yes, of course.

B All right. If there's nothing else?

45

A No, Professor. I have everything I need. Your staff has been very helpful.

B Perfect. I trust you'll be happy here at the University this semester.

A Yes. Yes, of course. Thank you for seeing me.

B We run a tight ship. I expect all hands on board.

School Principal and Parent

A Thanks for coming over on such short notice.

B Priorities. It's all about priorities in life.

A Glad you feel that way.

B My only child.

A I understand. And this isn't the first incident, as you should remember.

B Yes, I do remember.

A Well, I hope it will be the last. We certainly can't continue this way.

B The divorce has been a little hard for him these past few months. Maybe you could cut him a little slack.

A A little slack won't help him graduate.

B He's maintaining his grades, isn't he?

A Top of his class.

B That's good news, isn't it? I would think the school would be happy.

A It's the constant disruptions that are the issue. The reason I asked you here.

B Maybe he's bored. Not challenged by the curriculum. Not motivated by his teachers.

A It's not their job to motivate him. It's their job to present the curriculum and direct him through the system.

B Sounds very … mechanical.

A Preparation for the real world. What job doesn't require meticulous planning and minute attention to detail?

B The same kind of position that would benefit from free thinking and creative problem-solving.

A I'm wondering if your son gets his rebellious streak from you.

B I hope so. It's helped me launch three multimillion dollar businesses.

A I think we're done here.

B We are done here. I'm putting him in private school.

The Impostor Syndrome

A How's the new place? Getting settled in?

B More or less.

A More more or more less?

B About equal. Probably gonna be unpacking for the next six months.

A Welcome to the wonderful, terrifying world of personal growth.

B What's that supposed to mean?

A Moving up in the world, moving up in your career, moving up in your finances … is never convenient.

B Biggest place I ever lived in. I keep looking around and asking … how in the world did I get here?

A You're happy you bought the place, right?

B Some days yes. Some days … not so much.

A That's the Impostor Syndrome.

B The … what?

A The Impostor Syndrome. Feeling unqualified to do something you've just done. Feeling unworthy to enjoy something you've just accomplished.

B Yeah, maybe. I keep wondering how I'm gonna furnish the place, decorate the place … all that fun stuff I never had to think about before.

A The pesky little minutiae of human existence.

B Right on the money.

A Impostor syndrome. My Uncle John struggled with Impostor Syndrome his whole life. Had money in the bank but never enjoyed it.

B My mom and dad are the same way. Grew up in poverty. Doing better now, but they still have trouble spending money on anything.

A It's like walking around with your umbrella open because it rained yesterday.

B Man, that's a good one.

A Gotta leave the old you behind. You're not living in a studio apartment anymore. Time to step up your game and think bigger.

B This is just what I needed to hear today.

A We all do. No more thrift store furniture, either. Your new place is too nice for that.

B Got it. Come on, let's grab some lunch.

A Sure thing. You're buying.

B That's right. I'm buying.

An Existential Crisis

A   Hello.

B   Sorry … I didn't know anyone was here. Have you been here long?

A   Yes. I was here for several hours by myself when I had this epiphany.

B   Is that good or bad?

A   Both at the same time.

B   I think I … have no idea what you mean.

A   As a young person … middle school age, I suppose … I felt like I didn't fit in. I didn't really know what I was going to do when I got older.

B   I think a lot of young people feel the same way.

A   I've always had a slight existential crisis.

B   What do you mean?

A   Exactly! I kept asking myself … even as a child … what does this all mean? Why are we here on this planet? What is our greater significance? How are we connected to the myriad other life forms scattered throughout the galaxy?

B   That's the sixty-four thousand dollar question, isn't it?

A   Precisely! What's the purpose of life and how do we recover knowledge?

B   You mean like archaeology?

A No! Wisdom of the world as it was revealed to the ancients. The hidden primeval truths referenced in the Sumerian tablets. The unmistakable trail of breadcrumbs leading directly back to the Anunnaki.

B Yeah, I guess. I heard those guys could really fry chicken.

A They'll fry us if we remain asleep to the truth!

B I know. You gotta keep your head on a swivel nowadays.

A Stay strong. Wait for the sign. Key players will reveal themselves at the appointed time.

B Okay. But is it all right if I DVR the game? I like to fast forward through the commercials.

Learning to Relax

A What should we do next?

B Do we always have to do something?

A Yeah. Time is money.

B Can't we just … be?

A I don't understand the question.

B I guess what I'm trying to ask is … if you're always racing to the next moment, then what happens to the one you're living in right now?

A That's our preparation time. Vitally important to hit our next goal. The essence of entrepreneurship.

B Does everything have to be about our entrepreneurship?

A I think so. Human beings are natural creativity machines. We're at our creative best when we're actively pursuing that next goal or big idea.

B I'm not so sure about that. The best ideas reveal themselves in our moments of calmness and clarity. That's when we're best able to receive them.

A Sorry, mon ami. Great ideas don't interrupt you. You've got to pursue them.

B Can't pursue them on an empty tank. Sometimes we need to stop and recharge the ol' batteries.

A I have a self-charging battery. It's a hybrid, just like a Prius. Recharges itself in a continuous feedback loop.

B Have you ever considered yoga?

A Thought about buying a yoga studio once, but the numbers didn't quite work out. Ran a feasibility study and the neighborhood didn't support the investment yet. Gentrification was about three years off.

B No! I mean did you ever try yoga classes yourself?

A Me?! No. Why?

B You might have to learn how to relax.

A I kinda don't think so. Rolling around, stretching on a sweaty mat with a bunch of other sweaty people? Probably not for me.

B There are all kinds of other techniques. Meditation. Reiki. Tapping. The Release Technique. Emotional freedom technique. The Sedona method. Lots of different methodologies out there.

A Stop riding unicorns. We live in the real world. I don't have time to go to Burning Man to help you look for a left-handed monkey wrench.

Fast Day. Cheat Day.

A Wanna get lunch?

B Can't. I'm fasting.

A But you're not heavy. You look great.

B Thank you.

A So why are you fasting?

B General health principles. Everybody needs a little rest. And every body system needs rest. Our digestive systems need to recover from all the stress and mess we put them through daily.

A Stress and mess?

B Have it your way. Call it what you will.

A No, no … stress and mess sounds about right. Pretty accurate. My eating habits definitely have not been the best lately.

B What did you have for breakfast?

A Pancakes, three eggs, sausage links, cheddar cheese biscuits, and a cinnamon roll.

B Anything else?

A Two more cinnamon rolls.

B Really?

A I like cinnamon rolls.

B Stress and mess.

A How long have you been fasting?

B Couple months. I fast one day a week now.

A How did you start?

B I read a book about it ten years ago. Finally decided to try it out.

A How do you feel?

B About a million times better.

A Really?

B Maybe a billion. But I also have a cheat day … so I never feel deprived.

A That's a good idea.

B Everything in moderation. And you know what else?

A What else?

B I always have cinnamon rolls on my cheat day.

A Really?

B Uh-huh. I like cinnamon rolls too.

A I knew it.

B And I have a lot more than three of them.

A I'm liking this principle more and more.

Taking My Brother to Lunch

A Wanna get something to eat?

B Can't. Taking my little brother out to lunch.

A Good for you. Is he doing better these days?

B Little by little. He's been through a lot.

A Yeah, I know. I'm glad you're keeping an eye on him.

B Gotta. When he lost his money, he lost half his friends.

A What about the other half?

B They don't know he lost it yet.

A He's young. He'll bounce back.

B Hope so.

A Can I ask a … slightly uncomfortable question?

B Uh, yeah … I guess so.

A About how much money did he lose when all that mess went down?

B Not sure. I try not to ask him too many personal questions.

A Probably a good idea.

B I try to mind my own business.

A I try to do that too.

B Good thinking.

A Thank you.

B There's two reasons people don't mind their own business.

A What's that?

B No mind and no business.

A Got it.

B Good.

The Way of All Flesh

A Where you been?

B Oh, just … taking care of some family stuff.

A Little brother again?

B No, my grandmother. She's not doing so well these days.

A What's going on with her?

B Nothing going on. Just … old.

A Got it.

B Want to spend as much time with her as I can. For as long as I can.

A Yeah. Wish I spent more time with my grandma when I had the chance.

B I know what you mean. It's not easy watching them go down-hill.

A We'll all get there. The way of all flesh.

B I guess you're right.

A Doesn't make it any easier though … watching it happen right before your eyes.

B I know. My grandmother was an Olympic medalist back in the day. Now she can barely walk across the room by herself.

A That's rough. You're right. It's rough to watch them go down-hill.

B But it's not about me … and my reaction. It's about being there for her. I know she'd be there for me as much as she could if our roles were reversed.

A Good way of looking at it.

B She's a really great lady, honestly. Probably the coolest person in our family. Even if she's wasn't my grandmother, I'd still want to be friends with her.

A That's great. What do you do when you visit?

B Believe it or not, I try to make her feel young again.

A How do you do that?

B I find old TV shows that she used to watch back in the day. Not just *I Love Lucy*, either. I found shows that haven't been on TV in thirty or forty years.

A Not even reruns?

B Not even reruns.

A That's really cool.

B Yeah. It's not her fault she got old.

A We'll all get there. Hopefully, anyway.

B The way of all flesh.

The Application

A Did you send that thing in yet?

B No, I did not.

A Why not?

B I'm not even sure I want to go through with it now.

A There might be a deadline to apply.

B There is. It's coming up.

A You don't have to take the job if you don't want it.

B I know, I know.

A But you may as well apply so you have the option.

B No. I started, but it's taking me forever. It's kind of a hassle pulling all the documentation together for this job.

A Isn't it a hassle pulling money out of your savings and running up your credit cards trying to meet your bills every month?

B You don't have to say it like that.

A Sorry, I think it's better to be over-employed than under-employed.

B Maybe. I think I may just need more time.

A Guess what? We all do. But we all get the same twenty-four hours.

B I'm just feeling a little under-motivated these days, that's all.

A Feelings are not facts.

B That's a good one, but it's not making me like this job application any better.

A Okay, then maybe this job is not a good match for you. Are you still working your side hustle?

B A little.

A Come on, what's going on with you lately?

B I don't know.

A But, if you did know, what would it be?

B Maybe it's the wrong side hustle.

A Explain.

B I heard it said that when you climb the ladder of success, you better make sure you've got your ladder up against the right building.

A Man, that's a good one.

B Thank you.

A Tell you what. Do the application anyway. I'll help you move the ladder if you have to.

B Thanks. I'll send it in tomorrow.

A Tomorrow?

B No. Today.

Job Interview

A   How long were you in the military?

B   Not long enough.

A   Haven't heard too many applicants tell me that.

B   Things seemed to make more sense there.

A   More than on the outside?

B   Much more.

A   How so?

B   Specificity. No confusion as to chain of command.

A   No problem following orders then?

B   So far, so good.

A   Why'd you leave the military then?

B   Irreconcilable differences.

A   With your superiors?

B   In a manner of speaking.

A   Explain the manner.

B   They were my supervisors. Not my superiors.

A   Lot of that in the civilian world too, you know.

B   Understood. But supervisors in the civilian realm don't have quite as much firepower at their disposal.

A   Understood. Well … what type of work do you feel would best suit you?

B I like to shoot weapons and blow things up.

A That might limit your options.

B I don't believe in limitations. We live in an abundant world.

A Ever work construction?

B A little. Summers when I was in high school.

A Lot of openings right now. Buildings popping up everywhere. They do demolition work too. Hard work. Weekly pay.

B Sounds good to me.

A Can you get over there in the morning? Meet the crew chief?

B Count me in.

A Just put my mind at ease on something first.

B Fire away.

A Dishonorable discharge?

B How'd you guess?

A Been doing this a long time. You learn to read people.

B Do I still get to meet the crew chief?

A Yeah. This day and age … seems like anything goes. They allow things that would have disqualified someone years ago.

B Glad to hear it.

A How'd you manage to get yourself a dishonorable discharge? That's not easy to do.

B From people asking me too many questions.

How's the Job?

A How's the job?

B Meh. It's a job. Steady paycheck. Insurance.

A Doesn't sound like you like it very much.

B Beggars can't be choosers.

A Stop choosing to be a beggar.

B It's all right. Pays the bills. I'm not complaining.

A What happened to that idealistic, big thinking entrepreneur I knew in college?

B Still there. Back burner.

A Nobody ever changes the world from the back burner.

B Gotta have my safety net.

A Nothing's more dangerous than a safety net.

B What the heck is that supposed to mean?

A Safety's not safe if it keeps you from doing what you're supposed to be doing with your life.

B Guess I'm just not ready to step out into the unknown. Not yet.

A You know the old saying. A ship in the harbor is safe, but that's not what ships are made for.

B How'd you get so smart?

A By challenging myself.

B Challenging yourself how?

A To face the devil I don't know … instead of tolerating the devils I've known all my life.

B Yeah … but it's comfortable where I am.

A You're not here to be comfortable. You're here to be exceptional.

B Well … I guess the way to do that …

A Is to make yourself uncomfortable.

Welcome Back

A   Welcome back.

B   Thanks very much.

A   It hasn't been the same here without you.

B   It's good to be back.

A   Sorry the other position didn't work out.

B   I'd say they … were looking for a different type of employee.

A   What type is that?

B   One who doesn't mind bending the rules.

A   Ethics are a funny thing. They can really get in the way when you're in the wrong place.

B   Well, I'm very happy to be back in the right place.

A   Nobody here's gonna ask you to break the law. Or even bend it.

B   I know that.

A   But that temptation is hard to resist. That was a lot of money they were throwing your way.

B   The money was fine … but not enough for what they wanted.

A   Believe me, I understand that temptation. I've been there myself.

B   Where do you go to get your character back after you've sold it to the highest bidder?

A Well, you won't have to worry about that any more. We kept your desk just like you left it.

B You … didn't hire anyone new to fill my spot?

A No. I had a feeling you'd be back.

B How did you know that?

A Well … I went to work for those guys once upon a time too.

B Gotcha. Sorry to hear that.

A Yes, I was sorry, as well.

Former Co-Workers

A Want a burger?

B You shouldn't grill 'em so close to the flame. Dries 'em out.

A That's the way I've always done it. They always turn out all right.

B It's like anything else. You get out of it what you put into it.

A Yeah. That's why they always turn out all right.

B Whatever you say.

A How's the new job treating you?

B It's a job. How about you?

A About the same. We miss you over there.

B Is that evil, twisted, malicious, deranged psychopath still working there?

A Which one? We have so many.

B That big, tall creep. What's his name? McKenzie.

A Uh … McCloskey?

B Right, right, right. McCloskey. Must have blocked his friggin' name from my mind.

A Yeah, he's still there. Probably a lifer.

B Hate to admit it, but that's why I left.

A You're not the first. That's why a lot of people left.

B Life's too short. Onward and upward.

A That's the goal.

B Got bigger and better things to do with my life.

A I hear you.

B Not my circus. Not my monkeys.

A You always had a way with words.

B Like to share a few words with that McCloskey jerk.

A Nah. He's not worth it. Focus on the good stuff in front of you, not the bad stuff behind you.

B Thanks. Much better idea.

A Let me share a few words with you, though … from Frank Sinatra. "The best revenge is massive success."

B Oooo … I like that.

A Good. Focus on more of what we like. Less of what we don't like. Better for you, me, and the whole world.

B And a whole lot better for McKenzie.

A McCloskey.

B Right. Whatever.

Got a Cigarette?

A Got a cigarette?

B Thought you quit.

A Soon. Got a cigarette?

B Yeah … but it's my last one.

A Can I have a drag?

B Maybe it's time you quit.

A Maybe it's time you shut up, light up, and give me a drag.

B You might have to work on your attitude.

A I can't smoke an attitude. Come on, light one up for me.

B It's bad for you.

A Who are you, the Surgeon General?! It's bad for both of us.

B I've got mine under control. I only smoke three … maybe four a day. One pack lasts me a week or more.

A Congratulations. Now take one out of next week's pack and light it up for me.

B Not so loud. You're attracting attention. Everybody's looking at us now.

A Good. Maybe somebody's got a cigarette.

B Okay, okay, you win! Here, take it! Take my last one!

A Really?

B Yeah, I just quit. Happy now?

71

A Very. Thanks.

B My pleasure. Say hello to the Surgeon General for me.

A I'll be happy to.

B Great. Enjoy.

Did You Bring the Money?

A You're on time.

B Yeah.

A Did you bring the money?

B Not exactly.

A That's not what we like to hear.

B Believe me … I didn't enjoy saying it.

A We have two possible responses to the question I asked you. "Yes" and "Yes, I've got it all right here. Just like you asked. Cold, hard cash." Understand?

B Yes … I understand.

A Good. I repeat: Did you bring the money?

B No.

A What am I gonna do with you?

B Give me another month?

A That's not what I was thinking.

B There's another option.

A Enlighten me.

B You can drop to your knees and lie down quietly. Face down, with your hands behind your back.

A Now why would I do that?

B To show the nice police officer standing behind you that you're not going to give us any trouble. He's looking a little trigger happy right now.

A There's no police officer standing behind me.

B Sure about that?

A Sure about that.

B That's not what we like to hear. He's all yours, Sergeant.

A Nice try. But I'm not turning around.

B Suit yourself. Cuff him.

Empty Threats. Full Meaning.

A   Good to see you.

B   Good to be seen.

A   Didn't think you'd show up.

B   You didn't think.

A   There's two ways this can go.

B   Is one of them the hard way?

A   Let's hope it doesn't come to that. I'm here to make sure we avoid any further unpleasantries.

B   Can I share something with you?

A   Please. I love to share. I live to share.

B   I've been around a long, long time.

A   I can see that.

B   And I've been threatened a time or two in my life.

A   Sorry to hear that.

B   You will be. Because when someone threatens me … they only do it once.

A   It would appear we are at an impasse.

B   I'm never at an impasse. I'm always moving forward.

A   Well then, let's take this conversation outside, shall we?

B   Yes, more room to move.

A Enjoy it while you can. You won't be moving for long.

B Famous last words.

A If you say so. Shall we?

B Surely.

A Knock at the Door

A Good evening.

B Can I help you, officer?

A No, I saw the lights on and just thought I'd check. Make sure everything's okay.

B Just fine, thank you. I work late sometimes. Hope the lights aren't disturbing the neighbors.

A No, but it's a lot of lights. Are you working in every room of the house?

B No, of course not. Just a little careless, I guess.

A Hey, we've all been there.

B I'll shut them off. No sense making the electric company rich.

A Yeah, I know what you mean.

B Anything else I can do for you?

A No, no, I'm just checking because I saw the lights and didn't recognize the car in the driveway.

B Well, thank you again, officer. I'll get back to my work. Deadlines, deadlines, deadlines. You know how it is.

A Are you a friend of the owners?

B Relative actually. Cousin from out of town.

A Whereabouts?

B Oh, not too far. Just housesitting while my relatives are away.

A Will the Millers be home soon?

B I don't know the Millers. My cousins' name is Madison.

A Oh, yes, Madison, of course. Got the names mixed up. I have so many houses on my patrol.

B Well, if there's nothing else?

A Have a good evening.

B Good evening, officer. Stay safe out there.

Where's Jimmy?

A Where's Jimmy?

B Gone.

A Excuse me?

B Jimmy doesn't live here anymore.

A What?!

B He's been gone a long time.

A Can't be that long. I just saw him a couple of months ago.

B Yeah, well … a lot can happen in a couple of months.

A Any idea where he went? Do you have his new address?

B Nope. And nope.

A This is a little embarrassing, but … he owed me money.

B Get in line. Jimmy owed everybody money.

A He did?

B Why do you think he's gone?

A Oh, man … what about that business he was running?

B Did you ever meet any of those high rollers he was supposedly working with?

A Uh, come to think of it … no. No, I didn't.

B I don't think he did either. The whole story was fiction, apparently. All a big show. Smoke and mirrors.

A   Pretty convincing … for a show.

B   He was slick. Who knows? Maybe he believed it all himself.

A   Guess I'm eating crackers for a while. That was all the savings I had.

B   My money went south too. I'll be switching to a cheaper brand of caviar.

A   Sorry to hear it.

B   Can I offer you some unsolicited advice … from someone who's been down this road a few times before?

A   Yeah, sure.

B   There's no such animal as something for nothing. And if it sounds too good to be true, it probably is.

A   Yeah. Good advice.

B   My dear, departed dad said it best. The safest way to double your money is to fold it in half and put it back in your pocket.

Evacuate the Building

A Sorry. I didn't know anyone was in this room.

B I just checked in yesterday.

A I'll have to ask you to leave.

B Leave? But I just checked in.

A We're relocating everyone on this floor.

B May I ask why?

A I believe it may be a safety issue.

B What kind of safety issue?

A Sorry, I'm not at liberty to say.

B Why is that?

A Uh … it's confidential information.

B I'm here as a guest. I have a right to know. It involves me.

A There might be a gas leak.

B Damn! Why didn't you say so in the first place?

A I didn't want to alarm you.

B You're alarming me more by not saying so in the first place.

A Sorry. I just started this job. I never evacuated a building before.

B Okay, You gotta let people know certain things.

A Sorry. Can I help you pack? Get your things together?

B You already said sorry. Don't keep saying sorry.

A Sorry.

B Don't be sorry. Just be better.

A Yeah. Yeah … okay.

B How about you? Do you need help?

A No.

B Are you sure?

A No.

B Do you need help evacuating this building?

A Uh, yeah, maybe. This is a little stressful for me.

B It would be stressful for anyone. Come on. Let's go. We got this.

More Right Than Wrong

A   I think there's something wrong with me.

B   There's more right with you than wrong with you.

A   How do you know that?

B   Because there's more right with the world than wrong with the world. Have faith. Stay strong. Better days are coming soon.

A   But how do you know that?

B   Trust me. I've been around and seen some things. And I know you're going to make it through this.

A   How do you know that?

B   From your prior history.

A   Repeat. How do you know that?

B   Because of everything you survived up until now. Positive proof that you've got resilience and tenacity.

A   Maybe so.

B   Definitely so. Resilience and tenacity go a long way. A lot more than you can imagine.

A   Thanks. It's nice to know that someone sees my potential.

B   I see more than your potential. Potential is theoretical. Experience is practical. I see your results. You're battle-tested, battle-scarred, and battle-proven.

A   Wow. Well … thank you for that.

B And I'm looking forward to hearing stories about your next victory. Even if it's just a little one. Even if it's just another tiny victory over yourself.

A I think this is making a lot of sense now. Baby steps.

B Exactly. Baby steps. Some days you just put one foot in front of the other.

A Easy does it, right?

B Yep. Start moving forward. Stop moving backward.

Unlikely. Implausible. Impossible. True.

A I can't believe any of this. You've got to be kidding me.

B I know it's not what you were expecting … or even what you wanted to hear.

A Just think about what you're saying. How am I supposed to believe any part of this story?

B I'm telling you … that's exactly the way it happened.

A But it doesn't even make sense.

B It doesn't have to make sense. It's factually accurate. Many things that are implausible don't have to make sense because they really happened.

A You're talking in circles.

B That's because our world is round. I'm trying to show you how it works.

A All of this is fine and well and good. But it doesn't change the fact that what you're telling me is impossible. It could not possibly have happened. It defies the laws of physics.

B Oh, ye of little faith.

A I am a scientist. I am a natural skeptic. I believe a fifth of what I see and another fifth of what I'm told.

B Would you care to take a little trip down the road with me and see for yourself?

A Are you telling me you have proof?

B Yes, physical proof in my storage unit down the road. Safe from prying eyes.

A Ah, yes, the famous storage unit.

B Right. And you'll need that fifth when you see what's in there. You're going to need a good, strong drink.

A All right, let's see what you've got in that top-secret storage unit of yours.

B Some people just gotta learn the hard way.

Mystery Girl

A   What do you make of this one?

B   This one is a puzzlement. Any bright ideas?

A   Not much to speak of. Victim came in late last night. Deceased maybe forty-eight to seventy-two hours.

B   Sounds about right. Cause of death is a little more mystifying.

A   Trying to avoid a full autopsy, but we may just have to go that route.

B   I suppose. I'm guessing it wasn't natural causes.

A   Agreed. Got a name?

B   No. No personal belongings. No purse. No wallet. No ID.

A   Did you print her?

B   Yeah. No matches anywhere.

A   Nothing? Nothing international? Visas, passports, foreign work permits?

B   Zero, zero, and zero. It's like she popped in out of thin air just to show up dead in our little town.

A   Very thoughtful of her.

B   Funny, I was thinking the same thing.

A   But how did she end up on that mountain?

B   No burns. No scrapes. No rips or tears on the back of her clothing. She wasn't dragged.

A No tire tracks up there, either. She wasn't dumped.

B No scars, cuts or abrasions. No blood, skin, or residue under the fingernails.

A Where's Sherlock Holmes when you need him?

B Sitting this one out.

A I don't blame him.

B No bruises or contusions on her face or body. No blunt force trauma.

A No needle marks. No obstructions in her throat.

B What does that tell you?

A Our mystery girl knew her killer.

B Right. And her killer knew what he was doing.

Agent Cassidy Meets Agent Miller

A Agent Cassidy?

B I'm Cassidy.

A Miller. Glad you're here. Reputation precedes you.

B We do what we can, Agent Miller. We hope for good results.

A I hear you've had plenty of good results.

B We do what we can.

A You're familiar with our case?

B Yes. Agent Tessler debriefed me.

A Good. You saw the new photographs?

B Very disturbing. Also very instructive.

A Frankly, we're stumped. Hoping you'll have some ideas.

B I do, but you won't like them.

A Try me.

B You need a decoy.

A We tried that a month ago.

B I know. You used the wrong bait.

A Meaning?

B Ever go fishing, Agent Miller?

A Sure.

B Catch many?

A Plenty.

B What did you put on the hook?

A Worms.

B Do you like to eat worms?

A No, I do not.

B What do you like to eat?

A Steak.

B Why didn't you put steak on the hook?

A It's not about me. It's about the fish.

B Exactly. Stop thinking like a logical, clear-headed law enforcement professional. Start thinking like an evil, deranged, twisted sociopath.

A I like where you're going with this.

B Good. You'll like it even better when I bring in your killer. Then you can buy me that steak.

A Steak? I'll buy you the whole damn cow.

B Looking forward to working with you, Miller.

A Looking forward to good results, Cassidy.

You're Late Again

A Uh … what time is it?

B You're late. Again. Twenty minutes.

A Yeah, sorry. Hope it's not a big deal.

B It is a big deal. I'm running a business not a bingo game.

A Yeah, sorry. Car trouble.

B Really? That's what you told me last week.

A Same car. Same trouble.

B Might want to up your game a notch.

A What do you mean?

B I mean get your act together.

A I am.

B You're not. Show me you want to be here. Show me you can make it to work on time.

A I'm saving up for a new car. I'm just not there yet.

B You don't need a new car. You need a new attitude. A can-do attitude. Get a rental. Take the bus. Take the train. Ride a scooter for all I care. Just get yourself here on time from now on. Got it?

A Yeah, but it's not—

B It's not what?

A I don't know—

B You don't know what?

A I can't—

B You can't what?! There's no can't! No more excuses! From 8 AM to 5 PM, your hind end belongs to me.

Three in the Morning

A Did you hear about Alex and Pat?

B What about them?

A I heard they're splitting up.

B Again?

A I think it's for good this time.

B You think or you know?

A I think I know.

B It's always more credible if you know what you think.

A No, no, no. Don't put that mess on me. I was there last night until three in the morning. Trying to calm them both down.

B They were fighting again?

A Big fight. Four cops.

B Oh! I didn't know it went that far.

A So far there's no turning back.

B What's the best way we can help?

A I don't have the answer.

B But if you did have the answer, what would it be?

A Maybe steer them towards couples counseling?

B After steering them out of their police cars.

A What's your point?

B   Some people are not supposed to be married. We used to call them "mental health singles."

A   Mental health singles?

B   People who stay single to protect the mental health of the singles who would otherwise have married them.

A   Don't say it like that. There's worse things than being single.

B   Yes, being separated by four policemen answering a domestic disturbance complaint at three in the morning.

A   You don't have to say it like that.

B   I do have to say it like that. Apparently, that's how it happened.

What Do You Want?

A What do you want for lunch?

B I don't know. What do you want?

A I don't know. I asked you. What sounds good?

B Depends. What do you like?

A I like everything. You know that.

B Pizza?

A Perfect.

B Or we could do Chinese.

A My favorite.

B Italian would be nice.

A Great.

B Sushi?

A Sold.

B Tell me something.

A Okay.

B Why do I always have to come up with ideas and suggestions?

A Because you always have good ones.

B Thanks.

A Welcome.

B But you never contribute ideas. You never pick a place to eat.

A But I always pay.

B Money's not everything.

A Then why don't you pay?

B Because money's not everything.

A There you go.

B And here I stay.

A Are you saying you don't wanna go for lunch?

B I'm saying I'm hungry, but I don't want to pick the place any more.

A Then I don't want to pay any more.

B That's very narcissistic.

A Why am I narcissistic?

B Because finance is not my skill set.

A Okay. Deciding where to go is not my skill set.

B Yep. Classic narcissistic behavior.

A Look, let's start over.

B That's a really good idea.

A What do you want for lunch?

B I lost my appetite.

Deja Vu for Me and You

A Thanks for meeting me.

B Been a little worried about you.

A Thanks. Sometimes … I feel like I'm not me anymore.

B Yeah, I think I … kinda don't know what in the world you mean.

A Did you ever step into a room … in a brand new place …

B Yeah?

A And get the feeling you experienced something before?

B You mean like deja vu?

A Exactly.

B Didn't you just ask me that question?

A Come on. No jokes.

B Promise.

A And then sometimes when I watch old movies.

B Right.

A Do you ever watch old movies?

B No.

A Well, I look at all those people who lived way back before we were born … and feel like I can remember being there with them … once upon a time.

B Maybe you're just unusually empathetic.

A I don't think that's it.

B I do.

A I'm talking about experiencing a deep and profound sense of deja vu.

B How can you experience deja vu in a place you never visited before?

A I don't know. Maybe it's reincarnation. Extrasensory perception. Racial memory stored in the collective unconscious. I can't explain it. I only know when I'm experiencing it. It's a very specific feeling.

B Feelings are not facts.

A That doesn't make them any less potent.

B Who says you have to participate in every feeling that comes your way? Where is that written?

A Nowhere. But I want to make sure I'm not missing out on something I should be paying attention to.

B You should be paying attention to things on this Earth. Things that are real and physical and tangible.

A Not everything real is physical and tangible. Pablo Picasso said everything we can imagine is real.

B Well, he was out of his mind. Have you ever seen his paintings?

A No.

B They were weird. He was a little out there.

A Maybe the world needs people who are a little out there. Einstein said imagination is more important than knowledge.

B Einstein said that?

A Yes. Brilliant scientist. Was he out of his mind too?

B No, but I think I'm starting to experience that sense of deja vu myself.

A See? It's a universal experience across cultures! It demonstrates the commonality of human experience.

B Didn't you just tell me that?

Unofficial Guidelines

A   I think we need to establish some guidelines.

B   I thought we already had them. Our company SOP.

A   Right. Let's think of these as our unofficial guidelines … but guidelines just the same.

B   I'm not sure I understand your meaning.

A   I saw the couple you were talking to earlier today.

B   Yes, I think I'm going to close them. Great credit scores. Both working full time. And they loved the unit I showed them.

A   Keep showing the apartment. Not exactly the … demographic we're looking for.

B   Repeat. I'm not sure I understand your meaning.

A   Let's just say … they're not our kind of people.

B   I hope you're not saying what I think you're saying.

A   That's exactly what I'm saying.

B   What year is this? Are we living in the 1950s?

A   I don't think I appreciate your sarcasm.

B   And I don't think I appreciate your unofficial guidelines.

A   Remember what I said.

B   I won't forget it.

A   Good.

B   And neither will the housing commission.

Favorite Film?

A Favorite film?

B American or foreign?

A Both. Either. American films are foreign films when you travel overseas.

B Good point. Pre-war or post-war?

A Irrelevant. If you can't make a good movie in peacetime, you'll never make a good movie in wartime.

B They made *Casablanca* in wartime.

A American movie. It was still peacetime in Hollywood. Roosevelt didn't call up the troops until two years later.

B Point well taken. Comedy or drama?

A Drama.

B *Casablanca* is definitely up there.

A Agreed. And I'll add the John Huston film … *The Man Who Would Be King*. Michael Caine and Sean Connery killed it.

B Can't argue with you there. How about something more modern?

A *La La Land.*

B Solid choice. That's three winners right there. Drama.

A Your turn. Comedy?

B Not sure. *Dirty Rotten Scoundrels*, maybe.

A Good one. Michael Caine again. He's the best. What else?

B *The Hangover.* I love the part with Mike Tyson and the tiger.

A Me too. Somehow overlooked by the Academy that year.

B Best performance by a jungle cat in a major motion picture.

A One more comedy. I want three.

B *Some Like it Hot.* Marilyn.

A Best of the best. No time for the rest.

B Boom. Done.

Running Away Together

A Good to see you.

B Good to see you too. We really need to talk.

A I know. I've got a great idea.

B We've been seeing a lot of each other lately and …

A I've never been happier in my life.

B … uh, this is difficult.

A It doesn't have to be.

B I think we should take things slow and—

A I think we should run away together.

B No. That's not a good idea.

A It's a great idea.

B I'm not ready for this. I haven't really dated a lot of people.
I'm not comfortable getting this close this fast.

A What's the correct number? How many people are you supposed to date before you date who you're really supposed to
be with? Who you're supposed to run away with?

B I'm not running away with anyone. I want to take things slow
and get married when I'm good and ready.

A You're good now.

B But I'm not ready.

A I've got a full tank of gas and a cooler full of snacks and energy drinks.

B I think you've had enough energy drinks.

A You're my energy drink.

B My life is … planned.

A Our life together will be … an adventure.

B Adventures are for story books and fairy tales.

A C'mon, live a little. We'll be like Romeo and Juliet.

B They both died.

"Without involvement, there is no commitment.
Mark it down, asterisk it, circle it, underline it.
No involvement, no commitment."

Stephen Covey

Appendices

Afterword: Focus on Your Voice

Most actors speak too fast. Even though the scenes in this book feature rapid-fire dialogue, it's still important to vary your tone and learn to modulate your speech. When performing these scenes, always remember that your audience will be hearing these lines for the first time. Actors need to make sure that audiences hear and understand every word so that they don't miss an important story point. Make a conscious choice to find spots in every scene to slow down and vary the tempo of your delivery.

Remember, people who are in control never rush. Don't rush the way you walk or the way you talk—particularly at auditions. Take your time. Focus on giving your audience a performance worth waiting for. When you do that, they won't want you to rush though your dialogue. They'll want to listen actively, relish every delicious word, and appreciate your confident and nuanced interpretation of the scene.

Take your time. Focus on giving your audience a performance worth waiting for.

Voice-over actors are the real experts at this, but everyone working on stage and screen can learn these subtleties too. A class in voice-over technique can be extremely helpful—even if you don't want to work in audio book narration, commercials, or animation.

A voice-over class with a reputable instructor will teach you to vary your speech and show different levels of intent. Singing lessons will help you develop this identical skill—even if you have zero interest in performing in musical theater. Voice-over classes and singing lessons will help you vary the pitch and tone of your voice. This vocal skill expands your range. You can go lower to show confidence, romantic interest, or evil intentions. You can go higher to show nervousness, fear, or surprise.

I believe voice is the most under-utilized technique in the actor's toolbox. If you're looking for the simplest and most direct way to stand out from the crowd in your auditions and performances, then start focusing on your voice. After working on this diligently for six months, you won't even have to think about it anymore. It will become automatic. I can promise you that most of the other actors reading for your role overlook this important aspect of their training.

Also by Mike Kimmel

Adult

50 Secrets Nobody Tells You in Hollywood
Monologues for Adults
Monologues for Young Adults
The Actor's Book of Quotes
Six Critical Essays on Film

Teen

Scenes for Teens
Monologues for Teens
Monologues for Teens II
One-Minute Monologues for Teens

Children

Acting Scenes for Kids and Tweens
Monologues for Kids and Tweens
Monologues for Kids and Tweens II

Recommended Reading

Acting for Films and TV by Leslie Abbott

Acting in Film by Michael Caine

Acting in Television Commercials for Fun and Profit by Squire Fridell

Actions: The Actor's Thesaurus by Maria Calderone and Maggie Lloyd-Williams

The Actor's Life by Jenna Fischer

Adventures in the Screen Trade by William Goldman

The Alchemy of Acting: The Evolution of Craft in Film by Jim Blumetti

All About Me by Mel Brooks

An Actor Prepares by Constantin Stanislavski

An Agent Tells All by Tony Martinez

The Art of Acting by Stella Adler

Audition by Michael Shurtleff

The Backstage Actor's Handbook by Sherry Eaker

Being an Actor by Simon Callow

A Book by Desi Arnaz

The Business of Acting by Brad Lemack

Catching the Big Fish by David Lynch

The Courage to Create by Rollo May

The Dramatic Writer's Companion by Will Dunne

Dreams Into Action by Milton Katselas

Ego is the Enemy by Ryan Holliday

Entertainment in the Old West by Jeremy Agnew

Fame: The Hijacking of Reality by Justine Bateman

Film: An Illustrated Historical Overview by Andrea Gronemeyer

The First Frame by Steve McCarten

Screenplay by Syd Field

Free Play: Improvisation in Life and Art by Stephen Nachmanovitch

The Godfather Notebook by Francis Ford Coppola

The Great Movies by Roger Ebert

Greenlights by Matthew McConaughey

The Hidden Persuaders by Vance Packard

Hollywood by Charles Bukowski

Hollywood Babylon by Kenneth Anger

The Hollywood Survival Guide for Actors by Kym Jackson

How I Made a Hundred Movies in Hollywood and Never Lost a Dime by Roger Corman

How to Act and Eat at the Same Time by Tom Logan

How to Audition on Camera by Sharon Bialy

How to Avoid the Cutting Room Floor by Jordan Goldman

How to Get Ideas by Jack Foster

How to Make it in Hollywood by Linda Buzzell

How to Write a Movie in 21 Days by Viki King

Impro by Keith Johnstone

Improvisation for the Theater by Viola Spolin

In Such Good Company by Carol Burnett

It Would Be So Nice if You Weren't Here by Charles Grodin

Know Small Parts by Laura Cayouette

Leading with My Chin by Jay Leno

Live Cinema by Francis Ford Coppola

Love, Lucy by Lucille Ball

Making Movies by Sidney Lumet

Making Movies Work by Jon Boorstin

Meeting of Minds by Steve Allen

Mighty Minutes by Jim Hall

Movie Speak by Tony Bill

The Movie that Changed My Life by David Rosenberg

Much Ado About Me by Fred Allen

My Rendezvous with Life by Mary Pickford

Notes on the Making of Apocalypse Now by Eleanor Coppola

Number One is Walking by Steve Martin and Harry Bliss

Ogilvy on Advertising by David Ogilvy

On Screen Acting by Edward and Jean Porter Dmytryk

The 100 Greatest Advertisements by Julian Watkins

100 Years, 100 Stories by George Burns

A Pictorial History of the Silent Screen by Daniel Blum

The Power of Myth by Joseph Campbell

A Practical Handbook for the Actor by Melissa Bruder

Purple Cow by Seth Godin

Reading the Silver Screen by Thomas C. Foster

Rebel Without a Crew by Robert Rodriguez

Sanford Meisner on Acting by Sanford Meisner

Social Media for Actors by Heidi Dean

The Talent Code by Daniel Coyle

Tips: Ideas for Actors by Jon Jory

True Strength by Kevin Sorbo

Understanding Movies by Louis Giannetti

A View from the Middle by Larkin Campbell

Voice-Over 101 by Debi Derryberry

Who is Michael Ovitz? by Michael Ovitz

Wild Bill Wellman: Hollywood Rebel by William Wellman Jr.

Wishful Drinking by Carrie Fisher

About April Hartman

April Hartman has been in the film industry now for over twenty years. She started her journey as an actor and has ventured into producing and directing over the years. April now has over ninety professional credits on IMDb that include major TV series, film leads, stunts and more. She has filmed all over the United States and worked alongside some of the industry's most notable actors.

Through the festival circuit, April has had films flourish all over the United States and abroad including Cannes Film Festival, USA Film festival, Bare Bones Festival and many more. Not only have her films done extremely well, they have also earned her ten Best Actor nominations and seven Best Actor wins.

After conquering the Texas market, April moved to New Mexico for the rising film and television work. Since moving she has held multiple networking events to try and bring this growing community together. April believes strongly that no one person can do it all alone—and the more support, the better. To support this vision, she franchised the Texas-based Rack Focus Film Festival and produced a very successful Rack Focus Festival at the historic Lobo Theater in Albuquerque in 2025. This event helped many actors become first-time filmmakers, as well.

She is currently serving on the board of New Mexico Women in Film. Helping and supporting women in this industry is a passion of hers. April has also opened an acting school, Act Up Studios in Albuquerque to help actors in New Mexico become an unstoppable force! Act Up Studios offers classes for adults and teenagers, both in-person and online.

About Mike Kimmel

Mike Kimmel is a former pro wrestler and circus magician. Nowadays, he is a film, television, stage, and commercial actor and acting coach. He is a thirty-plus year member of SAG-AFTRA with extensive experience in both the New York and Los Angeles markets. He has worked with directors Francis Ford Coppola, Robert Townsend, Craig Shapiro, and Christopher Cain among many others. TV credits include *Game of Silence*, *Zoo*, *Treme*, *In Plain Sight*, *Cold Case*, *Breakout Kings*, *Memphis Beat*, *Suit Up*, *Buffy The Vampire Slayer*, and *The Oprah Winfrey Show*. He was a regular sketch comedy player on *The Tonight Show*, performing live on stage and in pre-taped segments with Jay Leno for eleven years. He also performed regularly with Gilbert Gottfried on USA Channel's comedic series *Up All Night*.

Mike has appeared in dozens of theatrical plays on both coasts, including Radio City Music Hall, Equity Library Theater, Stella Adler Theater, Double Image Theater, The Village Gate, and Theater at the Improv. He trained with Michael Shurtleff, William Hickey, Ralph Marrero, Gloria Maddox, Harold Sylvester, Wendy Davis, Amy Hunter, Bob Collier, and Stuart Robinson. He holds a B.A. from Brandeis University and an M.A. from California State University at Dominguez Hills. He has taught at Upper Iowa University, University of New Orleans, University of Phoenix, Glendale Community College, Nunez Community College, Delgado Community College, and in the Los Angeles, Beverly Hills, and Burbank, California public school districts. He is a two-time past president of New Orleans Toastmasters, the public speaking organization.

Mike has written and collaborated on numerous scripts for stage and screen. *In Lincoln's Footsteps*, his full-length historical drama on Presidents Lincoln and Garfield, was a semi-finalist in the National Playwrights Conference at the Eugene O'Neill Theater Center. Mike also received the Excellence in Teaching Award from Upper Iowa University and was a founding member of the Flambeaux Theater Company in New Orleans.

In 2019, the Independent Author Network selected his third book, *Monologues for Teens*, as their Performing Arts Book of the Year. In 2022, Best Indie Book Award (BIBA) honored *Monologues for Adults* as their annual winner in the performing arts category. Mike is also prominently featured in Francis Ford Coppola's groundbreaking book on his innovative theater-film hybrid process, *Live Cinema*.

Mike is a full voting member of the National Academy of Television Arts and Sciences, the organization that produces the Emmy Awards each year. He divides his time between Los Angeles, California and Albuquerque, New Mexico.

A Bold and Humble Request

If you've enjoyed *The Actor's Book of Scenes*—and feel that it would benefit our fellow actors and teachers—then please consider leaving a brief book review on the merchant site where you purchased it.

Book reviews are incredibly helpful for both authors and readers, particularly in a highly specific genre like the performing arts. Reviews help spread the word to readers looking for new material, and also help authors reach a wider audience.

https://amazon.com/review/create-review?&asin=B0GP9QV3Y8

The Actor's Book of Scenes

Additionally, we hope you'll consider recommending this book to your local public library or university library. Schools and libraries can often purchase books at a significant discount. In this way, the book can be made available to readers who are not able to purchase copies for themselves.

"Nothing in this world can take the place of persistence. Talent will not; nothing is more common than unsuccessful people with talent. Genius will not; unrewarded genius is almost a proverb. Education will not; the world is full of educated derelicts. Persistence and determination will always solve the problems of the human race."

CALVIN COOLIDGE

www.ingramcontent.com/pod-product-compliance
Lightning Source LLC
Chambersburg PA
CBHW060936050726

47592CB00003B/975